Painting History

Katacha Díaz

Illustrated by Linda Pierce

Tim and Lorenzo grew up
in a little town in **New Mexico.**
They liked school and sports.
And they loved to paint!

Tim and Lorenzo painted a mural.

It tells the story of their town.

A **mural** is a painting on a wall.

Tim and Lorenzo knew some things
about the town's past.
But they wanted to know more.
They went to the town's library.

They read about the town.
They also asked
many questions.

The boys learned
about the Spanish **settlers**
who came to the town.
The early Spanish settlers
planted grapevines.

They also built an **adobe** church.

Tim and Lorenzo thought of other things
that they liked about their town.
They liked the town's pretty mountains.
They also liked to see the dancing
at the special parties called *fiestas.*

The boys needed a drawing
to show all of their ideas.
Their drawing helped them
plan the mural.
Then they were ready to paint.

The mural had to cover a wall
in the police station.
Tim and Lorenzo began to paint,
using their drawings.
Fifth-grade students came
to help them.

After three months, Tim and Lorenzo
finished the mural.
It was six feet tall and six feet wide.
The boys used many cans of paint.
And they used lots of brushes.

Tim was proud of painting the mural.
Lorenzo said that it was also
a lot of fun.

Best of all, the two boys
were painting the history
of their town!

Glossary

adobe

mural

New Mexico

settlers